Book Index - Introduction to Artificial Intelligence

Preface

We live in an era of unprecedented technological transformation, where Artificial Intelligence (AI) has moved beyond the realm of science fiction to become an essential part of our daily lives. From movie and music recommendations to AI-assisted medical diagnosis, artificial intelligence is shaping how we interact with the world and each other.

Despite its growing presence, the concept of Artificial Intelligence remains a mystery to many people. How do intelligent systems work? What implications do they have for our society and the future of work? Should we be concerned about their impact on privacy and security? These are just a few of the questions that arise when discussing this technology.

This book has been written with the goal of providing an accessible and clear introduction to Artificial Intelligence, without requiring prior knowledge of computer science or advanced mathematics. We will explore its origins, various branches, and applications, as well as the challenges and opportunities it presents for the future.

Regardless of your background or level of experience, this book will help you understand the fundamentals of AI and its impact on different fields, from medicine to entertainment, education, and industry. The key is not only to understand how AI works but also how we can use it ethically and responsibly.

Welcome to this journey into the future of Artificial Intelligence.

Chapter 1: What is Artificial Intelligence?

Artificial Intelligence (AI) is a branch of computer science that aims to develop systems capable of performing tasks that normally require human intelligence. This includes image recognition, natural language processing, machine learning, and more.

1.1 Introduction to AI

We live in an increasingly technology-driven world, where Artificial Intelligence (AI) has become one of the most influential innovations. But what exactly is AI? Simply put, Artificial Intelligence is the ability of machines and computer systems to perform tasks that typically require human intelligence. This includes processes such as voice recognition, decision-making, pattern identification in data, and learning from experience.

Unlike traditional computer programs, which follow predefined instructions rigidly, AI systems can adapt and improve their performance over time through techniques such as machine learning.

Differences Between AI and Automation

It is common to confuse AI with automation, but they are not the same. Automation refers to systems programmed to perform specific tasks repeatedly, without the need to learn or improve over time. For example, a conveyor belt in a factory that moves products from one point to another is an automated system but not an intelligent one. In contrast, an AI used in the manufacturing industry could analyze production patterns, detect anomalies, and optimize processes without human intervention.

Why is it Important to Learn About AI?

Artificial Intelligence is already changing the world in multiple areas. Understanding it helps us:

Prepare for the future job market: Many industries are adopting AI to optimize processes and improve efficiency. Having knowledge of AI can be an advantage in the job market.

Make informed decisions: AI influences our daily lives, from algorithms that recommend content on social media to systems that approve bank loans. Knowing how these systems work allows us to be more critical and responsible users.

Understand challenges and risks: AI presents opportunities but also ethical challenges, such as data privacy and automated decision-making. It is crucial to understand these aspects to promote the responsible use of technology.

1.2 History and Evolution of AI

To better understand Artificial Intelligence, it is important to know its history and how it has evolved over time. Although AI has primarily developed in recent decades, its roots go back centuries to when philosophers and mathematicians began exploring the idea of mechanical intelligence.

Early Attempts to Create Artificial Intelligence

The concept of a "thinking machine" has been present in human imagination for centuries. From antiquity, myths and legends have described the creation of artificial beings with human-like capabilities. An example is the Greek myth of Talos, a bronze automaton created by Hephaestus to protect the island of Crete.

However, it was not until the 17th century that early thinkers began formulating concrete ideas about the possibility of artificial intelligence. René Descartes, for instance, proposed the idea that human thought could be broken down into mechanical processes, suggesting that one day it might be replicated in a machine.

Later, in the 19th century, Charles Babbage and Ada Lovelace developed the first concepts of computational machines. Lovelace even theorized that machines could go beyond mathematical calculations and manipulate symbols, which is considered one of the first ideas about the possibility of AI.

AI in the 1950s and the Rise of Computing

The true birth of Artificial Intelligence as a discipline occurred in the 1950s when advances in computing allowed scientists to develop the first theories and programs on AI.

One of the first milestones was the famous Turing Test, proposed in 1950 by British mathematician Alan Turing. In his paper *Computing Machinery and Intelligence*, Turing posed the question: "Can machines think?" To answer this, he designed an experiment where a human had to interact with another person and a machine without knowing which was which. If the human could not distinguish the machine from the other interlocutor, it was considered that the machine possessed intelligence.

During the same decade, the term "Artificial Intelligence" was officially coined in 1956 during the Dartmouth Conference, organized by John McCarthy, Marvin Minsky, Nathaniel Rochester, and Claude Shannon. This event brought together the first researchers in the field and marked the formal beginning of the discipline.

Key Moments in AI Development

Over the following decades, AI experienced periods of significant advances and crises due to technological limitations. Some of the most important milestones include:

1960s – Early AI Programs

- Development of the first expert systems, such as ELIZA, a primitive chatbot that simulated a conversation with a psychologist.
- Creation of the first machine learning algorithms.

1970s and 1980s – AI Winter

- Initial enthusiasm faded as computational limitations prevented expected progress.
- The first "AI winter" occurred, a period in which funding for AI research was drastically reduced.

1990s – AI Resurgence

- Improved computing power enabled advances in neural networks and machine learning algorithms.

- In 1997, IBM's Deep Blue supercomputer defeated world chess champion Garry Kasparov, demonstrating AI's potential in complex tasks.

21st Century – Modern AI and Deep Learning

- With the rise of Big Data and increased processing capacity, AI underwent a new revolution.
- Development of virtual assistants like Siri, Alexa, and Google Assistant.
- In 2016, AlphaGo, an AI program developed by DeepMind, defeated the world champion of Go, a game much more complex than chess.

Modern AI and Its Current Impact

Today, Artificial Intelligence is present in virtually all aspects of our lives. From recommendation systems on platforms like Netflix and YouTube to advanced medical diagnostics, AI is transforming entire industries.

Advances in deep learning and natural language processing have led to increasingly sophisticated models. Companies like Google, OpenAI, and Tesla are investing billions of dollars in AI research and development.

However, AI's evolution also presents significant challenges, such as ethics in job automation and data privacy. As technology advances, it is essential for society to participate in the discussion on how to regulate and use AI responsibly.

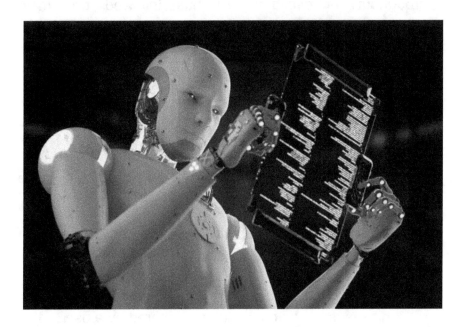

1.3 Fundamental Concepts of AI

Artificial Intelligence is a broad field that encompasses multiple approaches and techniques. To understand how it works and its applications, it is essential to become familiar with its key concepts. In this section, we will explore the differences between symbolic and data-driven approaches, machine learning, natural language processing, and other key topics.

Symbolic AI vs. Data-Driven AI

Throughout its evolution, AI has followed two main approaches:

Symbolic AI (or Rule-Based AI)

- Based on logic and reasoning through predefined rules.
- Uses expert systems that apply sets of rules to make decisions.
- Was the dominant approach in the early decades of AI.
- *Example:* A rule-based system for diagnosing diseases based on symptoms entered by a user.

Data-Driven AI (or Machine Learning)

- Relies on processing large volumes of data to identify patterns.
- Uses machine learning algorithms to improve over time.
- Has become the dominant approach today due to the availability of massive datasets and increased computing power.
- *Example:* A movie recommendation system that learns from user preferences.

Machine Learning

Machine learning (ML) is a branch of AI that enables machines to learn from data without being explicitly programmed for each task. There are three main types of machine learning:

Supervised Learning

- The model is trained with labeled data (i.e., where the correct answers are already known).
- Used in applications such as voice recognition and image classification.
- *Example:* A system that analyzes emails and classifies them as "spam" or "not spam" based on previous examples.

Unsupervised Learning

- The model looks for patterns in data without predefined labels.
- Used in customer segmentation or anomaly detection.
- *Example:* An algorithm that groups store customers into different categories based on their shopping habits.

Reinforcement Learning

- Based on a system of rewards and penalties to optimize an agent's behavior.
- Used in robotics, video games, and optimization systems.

Example: A robot that learns to walk by improving its movements through trial and error.

Artificial Neural Networks

Artificial neural networks are one of the foundations of deep learning, an advanced approach within machine learning. These networks are inspired by the structure of the human brain and consist of artificial neurons organized in layers.

The main characteristics of a neural network include:

- **Input, Hidden, and Output Layers:**
  - The input layer receives data.
  - The hidden layers process the information through mathematical computations.
  - The output layer generates a result based on the processed data.
- **Weights and Activation Functions:**
  - Each connection between neurons has a weight that is adjusted during model training.
  - Activation functions determine whether a neuron should be activated based on the data.

- **Training with Backpropagation:**
  - A method to adjust neural network weights by minimizing errors in predictions.

Example of application: Facial recognition on mobile phones, where the neural network analyzes facial features to unlock the device.

Natural Language Processing (NLP)

Natural Language Processing (NLP) is a branch of AI focused on the interaction between humans and computers through language. Its goal is to enable machines to understand, interpret, and generate text or speech.

Some applications of NLP include:

- **Automatic translation:** Google Translate uses AI to translate languages in real time.
- **Virtual assistants:** Siri, Alexa, and Google Assistant process voice commands and respond to questions.
- **Sentiment analysis:** Companies use AI to analyze opinions on social media and detect trends.

To achieve these advancements, NLP uses techniques such as:

- **Tokenization:** Dividing a sentence into individual words or phrases.

- **Lemmatization and stemming:** Reducing words to their base form for more efficient analysis.
- **Language models:** Algorithms like GPT (Generative Pre-trained Transformer) generate coherent texts based on the provided context.

Computer Vision

Computer vision is another key area of AI that allows machines to interpret and analyze images and videos.

Some applications include:

- **Facial recognition:** Used in security and biometric authentication.
- **Medical diagnosis:** AI analyzes X-rays to detect diseases.
- **Autonomous vehicles:** Self-driving cars use computer vision to identify traffic signs and pedestrians.

The computer vision process involves:

1. **Image preprocessing** (brightness adjustment, contrast, noise reduction).
2. **Feature extraction** (edges, shapes, colors).
3. **Image classification** using Convolutional Neural Networks (CNN).

Intelligent Agents and Decision-Making

An intelligent agent is a system that perceives its environment, processes information, and makes decisions to achieve a goal.

Examples of intelligent agents:

- A robotic vacuum that navigates a house while avoiding obstacles.
- A stock market algorithm that decides when to buy or sell shares.
- A chatbot that answers questions in an online store.

These agents can be:

- **Reactive:** Respond to immediate stimuli without learning from experience.
- **Goal-based:** Make decisions considering long-term results.
- **Learning-based:** Improve performance over time through data and past experiences.

Conclusion

The fundamental concepts of AI are essential for understanding how this technology works and why it is so powerful. From machine learning to computer vision and natural language processing, each of these elements allows AI to have a significant impact on society.

As we move forward in this book, we will see how these concepts apply to everyday life and different industries.

1.4 Applications of AI Today

Artificial Intelligence is no longer a futuristic concept; it has become a key tool in our daily lives. From virtual assistants on our phones to advanced medical diagnostics, AI is transforming multiple sectors. In this section, we will explore how AI is applied in various fields, with concrete examples of its impact.

Virtual Assistants and Chatbots

One of the most common uses of AI is in virtual assistants like Siri (Apple), Alexa (Amazon), and Google Assistant. These systems use natural language processing (NLP) to understand voice commands and respond to questions.

Examples of use:

- **Voice control:** You can ask Alexa to turn on the lights in your home or play music.
- **Quick responses:** Google Assistant can answer general questions, such as the weather or the news.

- **Agenda management:** Siri can schedule events on your calendar or send messages.

In addition to virtual assistants, chatbots are increasingly used on websites and social media to improve customer service. Companies like Meta (Facebook), WhatsApp, and Telegram employ chatbots to answer questions, provide technical support, and facilitate online purchases.

Impact:

- Reduced customer service wait times.
- Greater accessibility for people with visual or motor disabilities.
- Automation of repetitive tasks in businesses.

Artificial Intelligence in Social Media and Search Engines

Social media platforms such as Facebook, Instagram, Twitter, TikTok, and LinkedIn rely on AI to enhance user experience.

Examples of application:

- **Recommendation algorithms:** AI analyzes your interests and usage patterns to show you relevant content. For example, TikTok adjusts its "For You" section based on the videos you watch the most.

- **Content moderation:** Facebook and YouTube use AI to detect inappropriate content or fake news.
- **Facial recognition:** Instagram and Facebook identify people in photos and suggest tags.

Search engines like Google and Bing also use AI to improve search results and understand user intent. Thanks to technologies like RankBrain and BERT, Google can interpret complex queries and provide more accurate answers.

Impact:

- Better personalization of content on social media.
- Easier detection of fake news and hate speech.
- More intuitive and relevant searches.

Artificial Intelligence in Healthcare

The healthcare sector has been one of the most benefited by AI, with advancements in diagnosis, research, and patient care.

Examples of application:

- **Medical diagnosis:** AI algorithms can analyze X-rays, MRIs, and CT scans to detect diseases like cancer with accuracy comparable to or even greater than that of doctors.

- **Personalized medicine:** AI helps develop treatments tailored to each patient's genetic characteristics.
- **Virtual medical assistants:** Applications like IBM Watson Health provide recommendations to doctors based on clinical data.

Impact:

- Faster and more precise diagnoses.
- Optimization of doctors' time and cost reduction in hospitals.
- Greater accessibility to medical care in remote areas.

Artificial Intelligence in Finance and Banking

Financial institutions have adopted AI to enhance security, optimize investments, and offer more efficient services.

Examples of application:

- **Fraud detection:** Banks use AI to analyze transaction patterns and detect suspicious activity.
- **Financial assistants:** Applications like Cleo or Mint use AI to help users manage their personal finances.

- **Automated trading:** Algorithms known as "algorithmic trading" predict market movements and automatically execute buy or sell orders.

Impact:

- Reduction of fraud and increased transaction security.
- Access to automated financial advice.
- Greater efficiency in stock markets.

Artificial Intelligence in Education

The education sector has begun integrating AI to improve teaching and personalize learning.

Examples of application:

- **Adaptive learning platforms:** Applications like Duolingo and Khan Academy adjust lessons according to student progress.
- **Automated correction:** Tools like Grammarly use AI to detect writing errors and suggest improvements.
- **Virtual tutors:** Educational chatbots help students resolve doubts in real-time.

Impact:

- More personalized and accessible learning.
- Reduced workload for teachers.

- Greater student motivation through interactive teaching.

Artificial Intelligence in Transportation and Autonomous Vehicles

Transportation is another area where AI is revolutionizing the industry.

Examples of application:

- **Autonomous vehicles:** Companies like Tesla and Waymo develop cars that can drive without human intervention.
- **Traffic optimization:** Cities like Singapore use AI to manage traffic flow and reduce congestion.
- **Delay prediction:** Airlines and train companies use AI to forecast delays and adjust schedules.

Impact:

- Reduction of traffic accidents caused by human error.
- Greater efficiency in public transportation.
- Lower environmental impact through optimized routes.

Artificial Intelligence in the Entertainment Industry

AI has transformed the way we consume and create content.

Examples of application:

- **Personalized recommendations:** Netflix and Spotify use AI to suggest movies, series, and songs based on user preferences.
- **Content creation:** AI models like DALL·E and GPT can autonomously generate images, texts, and videos.
- **Video games:** AI improves gameplay by creating more realistic and dynamic NPCs (non-playable characters).

Impact:

- More immersive entertainment experiences.
- Generation of AI-created content.
- Development of more interactive video games.

Conclusion

Artificial Intelligence is present in almost every aspect of our lives. From healthcare to entertainment, its impact is undeniable and continues to grow at an accelerated pace. While AI has brought us great benefits, it also poses challenges, such as data privacy and its impact on employment.

In the next section, we will explore some of these challenges and debunk common misconceptions about AI.

1.5 Challenges and Misunderstandings About AI

Despite its advancements, Artificial Intelligence remains a field surrounded by myths and concerns. While some believe that robots will soon replace humans in all aspects of life, others see AI as an existential threat. However, beyond these perceptions, there are real challenges that need to be addressed, ranging from ethical issues to technological limitations.

In this section, we will analyze the main challenges and misunderstandings about AI, clearing up misconceptions and exploring the true problems that this technology faces.

Myths and Realities About Artificial Intelligence

There are many misconceptions about AI that stem both from science fiction and a lack of understanding about how it actually works. Below, we debunk some of the most common myths.

Myth 1: "AI is conscious and thinks like a human"

Reality: While AI can simulate human reasoning in certain tasks, it does not have consciousness, emotions, or intentions of its own. Current AIs are advanced mathematical systems that process information without truly "understanding" what they are doing.

Myth 2: "Robots will dominate the world and replace humans"

Reality: While automation has replaced certain jobs, AI remains a tool created and controlled by humans. Its development depends on political, economic, and ethical decisions.

Myth 3: "AI is infallible and always makes correct decisions"

Reality: AI makes mistakes and can be biased if trained with faulty or limited data. An AI system is only as good as the data it has been trained on.

Myth 4: "Any advanced software system is AI"

Reality: Not all automated software is AI. Many applications simply follow predefined rules without learning or adapting over time.

Ethics and Bias in Artificial Intelligence

One of the greatest challenges of AI is its ethical impact. As these technologies make decisions that affect millions of people, questions arise about their fairness and accountability.

1. **Bias in Data and Algorithms**

   AI learns from data provided by humans, meaning it can inherit and amplify existing biases. Some examples include:

   - **Discrimination in facial recognition**: It has been shown that some facial recognition AI systems have a higher error rate for darker-skinned individuals due to insufficient training data.

   - **Hiring bias**: Companies using AI to select candidates may end up favoring certain groups if historical data reflects prior discrimination.

2. **Accountability and Decision-Making**

   When an AI makes a mistake, who is responsible? This is a dilemma affecting sectors like healthcare and autonomous vehicles. Should the developer, the company using the AI, or the end-user be held accountable?

3. **Privacy and Data Security**

   Many AI systems require vast amounts of personal data to function properly. This raises concerns about:

- Protecting user information.
- Risks of data breaches or misuse.
- Mass surveillance and the loss of privacy.

Impact of AI on Employment

Automation has raised concerns about job loss in various sectors. However, the impact of AI on the labor market is more complex than it seems.

1. **Jobs at Risk**

   Some repetitive or routine tasks have been replaced by AI, such as:

- **Cashiers in supermarkets**: More and more stores are using self-checkout systems.
- **Basic customer service**: Chatbots have reduced the need for human operators in certain services.
- **Factory workers**: Robots have automated production in sectors like automotive manufacturing.

2. **New Job Opportunities**

   Although AI has eliminated some jobs, it has also created new professions, such as:

- Machine learning engineers.
- Data analysts.
- AI ethics specialists.
- AI experience designers.

3. **Adaptation and Retraining**

   To mitigate the negative impact on employment, it is essential that governments and businesses invest in education and training so that workers can acquire digital skills and adapt to the new labor market.

Technological Limitations of AI

Despite its advancements, AI still faces limitations that hinder its application in certain environments.

1. **Dependence on Large Volumes of Data**

   Most AI systems require massive amounts of data to train. Without sufficient data, models may be inaccurate or unreliable.

2. **Lack of Genuine Reasoning and Creativity**

   While AI can generate creative content, it lacks imagination and intuition like humans. Models such as ChatGPT can write coherent texts, but they do not "think" or "understand" like a person.

3. **High Costs and Energy Consumption**

   Training AI models, especially deep neural networks, requires significant computational power, leading to high costs and considerable environmental impact.

Regulation and Control of AI

Given the impact AI can have on society, many governments

are developing regulations for its responsible use.

Examples of regulation:

- **EU AI Regulation**: Aims to ensure transparency and prevent abuses in the use of algorithms.
- **Privacy regulations**: Laws such as GDPR in Europe establish rules regarding the collection and use of personal data.
- **Ban on facial recognition in some cities**: Some cities have restricted its use to avoid privacy violations.

The challenge lies in balancing innovation with protecting citizens' rights.

Conclusion

Artificial Intelligence is a powerful tool with enormous potential, but it also poses challenges that must be addressed responsibly. It is important to debunk myths and understand its true limitations and risks in order to use it ethically and safely.

In the next chapter, we will explore how AI is shaping the future and its long-term implications.

Chapter 2: The Future of Artificial Intelligence

Artificial Intelligence has transformed our society at multiple levels and will continue to play a key role in technological evolution. Although it has already revolutionized sectors such as medicine, industry, and commerce, experts agree that we are still in the early stages of its development.

This chapter will explore emerging trends in AI, its long-term impact on society, and the challenges we will face in regulating and ethically applying this technology.

2.1 Trends and Expected Advances in AI

Research in Artificial Intelligence is progressing at a rapid pace. Below, we examine some of the most promising innovations and how they could change the way we live and work in the coming decades.

General Artificial Intelligence (AGI): Is a Human-like AI Possible?

So far, all AI applications have been designed for specific tasks: translating texts, recommending movies, diagnosing diseases, or driving cars. These "narrow" AIs perform with great precision in their areas but cannot transfer their knowledge to other contexts.

The next major goal is to develop a General Artificial Intelligence (AGI), capable of understanding and learning any intellectual task in the same way that a human would. This would mean that the same AI could, for example, learn to program, play a musical instrument, understand human emotions, and solve abstract problems without needing to be specifically trained for each of these tasks.

If AGI were to be developed, its implications would be enormous. Some experts, such as computer scientist Nick Bostrom, warn that an AI capable of self-improvement could quickly surpass human intelligence and generate uncontrollable changes. Others, like Yann LeCun (Meta's AI expert), believe we are still far from achieving a system with human-like cognitive abilities.

When could we see AGI? Predictions vary: some researchers believe we could see significant advances in the next 20 or 30 years, while others argue that AGI is a purely theoretical concept and will never be achieved.

Explainable Artificial Intelligence: Towards More Transparent AI

One of the major issues with current AI systems is that they often function as "black boxes." This means that while they can make decisions with great precision, humans cannot always understand how they arrived at those conclusions.

This issue is especially critical in sectors like healthcare, banking, and justice. If an AI denies a loan or misdiagnoses a patient, it is essential to understand why it made that decision.

To address this issue, researchers are developing new explainable AI (XAI) techniques, which allow the visualization and understanding of the reasoning behind AI models.

An example of explainable AI is the LIME (Local Interpretable Model-agnostic Explanations) system, which analyzes the decisions of complex models and generates explanations understandable to humans.

AI and Robotics: The Rise of Intelligent Robots

The combination of AI and robotics will enable the creation of increasingly advanced machines. Some of the areas where we will see the greatest advances include:

- **Home assistance and elderly care**: Robots like Pepper have already been developed to interact with humans and provide companionship for the elderly or people with disabilities. In the future, we may see caregiver robots capable of assisting with household tasks and basic healthcare.

- **Industry and manufacturing**: Automation will continue to increase in factories. Robots like those from Boston Dynamics can already perform complex tasks such as carrying packages and navigating challenging environments.
- **Space exploration**: NASA and other space agencies are developing autonomous robots for exploring planets and asteroids. AI will enable these devices to make decisions in real-time without the need for human intervention.

Quantum Computing and Artificial Intelligence

Quantum computing is one of the most promising technologies of the future. Unlike traditional computers, which process information in binary form (0 and 1), quantum computers can perform calculations exponentially faster using qubits.

While we are still in the early stages of development, tech giants such as Google, IBM, and Microsoft are investing in the development of quantum computers with the goal of revolutionizing fields such as:

AI model optimization: Quantum computing could dramatically improve the speed and efficiency of machine learning algorithms.

Cybersecurity: Quantum systems will be able to develop encryption methods that are nearly impossible to crack, enhancing digital security.

Discovery of new materials and drugs: Quantum molecular simulation could accelerate the creation of new medicines and advanced materials.

2.2 AI and its Impact on Society

As AI becomes more powerful, its effects on society will become increasingly profound. Some of the most significant impacts include:

Transformation of the Labor Market

Automation has already replaced certain repetitive jobs, and this process is likely to continue. However, new opportunities will also arise.

Some jobs that could disappear or transform in the future include:

☐ Cashiers and salespeople: Self-checkout systems and AI in e-commerce will reduce the need for employees in physical stores.

☐ Public transport and freight drivers: Autonomous vehicles could replace many jobs in the transport sector.

At the same time, AI will create new professions, such as:

☐ AI and machine learning engineers.

☐ AI ethics specialists.

☐ Technicians for robot maintenance and supervision.

Education and Personalized Learning

AI-based educational systems will enable teaching to be adapted to each student's needs. Educational chatbots and virtual tutors will help students learn at their own pace, facilitating access to education worldwide.

AI Regulation and Ethics

The advancement of AI raises fundamental questions about its regulation. Who should control the development of these technologies? How can we prevent them from being used for malicious purposes?

Governments and international organizations are working on legal frameworks to ensure responsible use of AI. Some initiatives include:

- AI regulation in the European Union, which aims to guarantee transparency and prevent bias in algorithms.
- The ban on facial recognition systems in public spaces in several cities due to privacy concerns.

Conclusion

The future of AI is promising, but it also presents significant challenges. As technology advances, it will be crucial to find a balance between innovation and ethics, ensuring that its benefits reach society as a whole without compromising privacy, security, and human rights.

Chapter 3: AI and Human Creativity

When we think of creativity, we often associate it with the human ability to imagine, innovate, and express emotions through art, music, literature, and other forms of expression. However, Artificial Intelligence has begun to play an increasingly important role in these fields, challenging the idea that creativity is exclusively human.

In this chapter, we will explore how AI is transforming the world of art and culture, its current applications, and the ethical dilemmas it raises when used in creativity.

3.1 Can AI Be Creative?

Creativity has been considered for centuries as an exclusively human trait. However, recent advances in AI have shown that machines can generate music, write stories, paint pictures, and even design innovative products.

Defining Creativity: Human vs. Artificial

To understand the impact of AI on creativity, we first need to define what it means to be creative. In general terms, creativity involves:

- **Originality**: The ability to generate new and unique ideas.
- **Imagination**: The projection of abstract concepts beyond existing information.
- **Emotional Expression**: Creativity is often tied to human experience and the transmission of feelings.

Current AI models, such as DALL•E, GPT, and DeepDream, have demonstrated that machines can generate artistic content, but does this mean they are creative? The key difference is that AI does not have intention or consciousness; it simply identifies patterns in large volumes of data and generates results that mimic human art.

For example, an AI model trained on millions of paintings can produce a work of art resembling that of a famous artist, but it has no emotions or motivations behind its creation.

Difference Between Assisted Creativity and Autonomous Creativity

There are two main ways in which AI influences creativity:

1. **AI as an Assisted Tool**: In this case, AI helps humans create but does not replace their creativity. Examples include image-editing programs like Adobe Sensei or musical composition tools that suggest chords.

2. **AI as an Autonomous Creator**: Here, AI generates works without direct human intervention. An example is AIVA, an AI that composes music without the need for a human composer.

Both approaches are changing the way we understand the creative process and raise questions about the role of artists in a world where AI can produce original content.

3.2 AI in Visual Art: Painting and Generative Design

One of the most striking examples of AI in art occurred in 2018, when a painting created by an algorithm was auctioned at Christie's for $432,500. The work, titled Portrait of Edmond de Belamy, was generated by a machine learning model called GANs (Generative Adversarial Networks).

Generative Algorithms in Art

The most commonly used AI systems in art creation include:

- **DALL·E**: An OpenAI model that generates images from natural language descriptions.

- **DeepDream**: An AI developed by Google that transforms images into psychedelic landscapes based on neural networks.
- **Runway ML**: Software that allows artists with no programming knowledge to use AI to generate visual art.

Impact on the World of Design and Illustration

AI is revolutionizing graphic design and illustration in several ways:

☐ **Automatic logo and branding generation**: Tools like Looka or Brandmark can create customized logos in seconds.

☐ **Optimization of product design**: AI helps design innovative products by analyzing trends and generating new ideas.

☐ **Creation of virtual worlds**: In the video game industry, AI is used to design procedurally generated environments.

Although AI can accelerate creative processes, some designers fear that these technologies will reduce the demand for human illustrators and artists.

3.3 AI in Music: Composition and Automatic Production

Music is another area where AI has demonstrated surprising

capabilities. Companies like Google, Sony, and specialized startups have developed systems that can compose musical pieces in various styles.

Algorithms that Compose Music

Some of the most advanced AI systems in music creation include:

- **AIVA (Artificial Intelligence Virtual Artist)**: An AI trained to compose classical and cinematic music.
- **Magenta (from Google)**: An AI system that experiments with creativity in music and art.
- **Amper Music**: A tool used to create background music without the need for human composers.

Can AI Replace Musicians?

While AI can generate melodies and musical arrangements autonomously, the interpretation and emotional connection with the audience remain unique to human musicians. It is more likely that AI will function as a support tool in music production, rather than replacing artists.

3.4 AI in Literature and Creative Writing

Language models like GPT-4 have demonstrated an impressive ability to generate coherent and creative texts.

From article writing to novel creation, AI is changing the way written content is produced.

AI-Assisted Writing Tools

Some of the most popular AIs in this field include:

☐ **Sudowrite**: Assists writers with ideas and improvements to their texts.

☐ **ChatGPT**: Can generate stories, articles, and dialogues with a natural style.

☐ **Grammarly**: Helps correct grammatical errors and improve writing.

Can AI Write a Great Novel?

Although AI can produce structured narratives, emotional depth and genuine creativity are still traits exclusive to human writers. AI-assisted writing will be a powerful tool for authors and editors, but it is unlikely to replace the human sensitivity in literature.

3.5 The Ethical Debate: Should AI Be Recognized as an Artist?

As AI progresses in the creative field, ethical and legal questions arise:

Who is the true author of a work created by AI?

Should works generated by AI be protected by copyright?

Is it fair for AI to compete with human artists in contests and exhibitions?

Currently, intellectual property laws do not recognize AI as an author, so automatically generated creations cannot be protected by copyright. However, this legal framework could change in the future.

Conclusion

Artificial Intelligence is transforming creativity in all its forms, from painting to music and literature. While AI is a powerful tool for artists and creators, the essence of creativity still lies in human imagination and sensitivity.

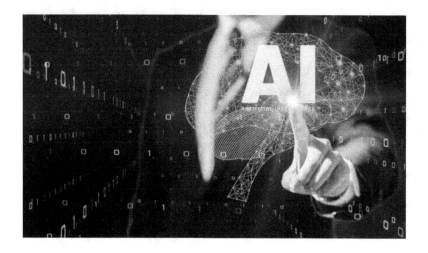

Chapter 4: AI and Ethics: Moral and Legal Challenges

The development of Artificial Intelligence has brought impressive advances, but it has also raised ethical and legal dilemmas. AI is not only used to improve efficiency in various sectors but also makes decisions that can profoundly affect people's lives. From discrimination in algorithms to mass surveillance, this chapter will explore the major ethical and legal challenges we face in the age of AI.

4.1 Responsibility in AI Decision-Making

One of the biggest ethical challenges in AI is determining who is responsible for its decisions. As algorithms make increasingly complex decisions, the question arises: what happens when an AI makes a mistake?

Cases where AI has made controversial decisions

Some examples of AI making problematic decisions include:

- **Predictive justice systems**: In the U.S., the COMPAS software, used to predict recidivism, has been criticized for biasing its evaluations against African American individuals.
- **Errors in autonomous driving**: Autonomous vehicles have been involved in fatal accidents, sparking debates about whether responsibility lies with the manufacturer, the vehicle owner, or the software.
- **Hiring algorithms**: Companies like Amazon have abandoned AI-based recruitment systems because they discriminated against women in hiring.

These cases show that while AI can be efficient, it is not free from errors and biases that can have serious consequences.

4.2 Bias in Artificial Intelligence

Why can AI be biased?

Bias in AI arises because models learn from historical data, which can contain human prejudices. For example, if a hiring algorithm is trained with data from a company that has historically hired more men than women, the AI is likely to replicate that bias.

Consequences of algorithmic bias

Bias in AI can lead to:

☐ **Discrimination in financial services**: Algorithms that grant loans may deny credit to certain groups for unjust reasons.

☐ **Inequality in healthcare**: AI models in healthcare may underestimate diseases in populations that are not well-represented in training data.

☐ **Prejudices in facial recognition**: Facial recognition systems have shown higher error rates in people with darker skin tones, leading to wrongful identifications and unjust detentions.

Solutions to mitigate biases

To reduce bias in AI, it is necessary to:

Use diverse and balanced data in training models.

Implement ethical audits and equity evaluations in algorithms.

Develop explainable AI systems that allow us to understand how models make decisions.

4.3 Privacy and Surveillance: The Dilemma of Data Usage

AI relies on large volumes of data, which has raised concerns about privacy and mass surveillance.

The use of personal data in AI

The collection and analysis of data have allowed the development of highly accurate models, but they have also opened the door to abuses in the handling of personal information. Companies and governments use AI for:

Targeted advertising: Platforms like Facebook and Google analyze our data to offer us ads tailored to our interests.

Facial recognition and surveillance: Governments in several countries have implemented AI systems to monitor citizens in public spaces.

Social media analysis: Algorithms can track posts and predict behaviors, raising questions about freedom of speech.

Regulations on privacy and data protection

To protect privacy, some regulations have been implemented globally:

☐ **General Data Protection Regulation (GDPR)**: In Europe,

this law establishes that citizens have the right to control how their data is used.

☐ **California Consumer Privacy Act (CCPA)**: In the U.S., this regulation gives users the right to request what data has been collected about them.

☐ **Bans on facial recognition**: Cities like San Francisco have banned the use of facial recognition in public spaces due to privacy concerns.

Despite these regulations, many companies continue to collect data on a massive scale, making privacy a central issue in the AI debate.

4.4 AI and the Impact on Employment

Will AI destroy jobs or create new ones?
One of the biggest fears about AI is its impact on employment. It is estimated that many professions will be automated, but at the same time, new jobs will emerge.

☐ Jobs at risk of automation:
• Cashiers and store employees
• Public and freight transport drivers
• Data analysts in repetitive tasks

☐ New job opportunities:

- AI and machine learning engineers
- AI ethics specialists
- Developers of robots and virtual assistants

The need for workforce retraining

To face these changes, it will be crucial to invest in education and training in digital skills. AI will not necessarily eliminate jobs, but it will change the nature of work.

4.5 AI Regulation: Challenges and Possible Solutions

How should AI systems be regulated?
Given AI's impact on society, it is essential to establish clear regulations. Some initiatives include:

- **AI ethics**: Companies like Google and Microsoft have developed ethical AI principles to ensure responsible use.
- **Government oversight**: The European Union is developing laws to regulate AI in critical sectors.
- **Algorithm transparency**: Efforts are being made to make AI models more understandable for humans.

Do we need AI with rights?

As AI advances, some experts have raised the possibility of granting legal rights to the most advanced systems. However, this sparks debate about whether machines can be considered "sentient beings" or if they should continue to be seen as mere tools.

Conclusion

AI ethics is a complex issue involving responsibility, privacy, bias, and its impact on employment. While AI offers enormous benefits, it is essential to establish regulations that ensure its fair and equitable use.

Chapter 5: AI in Everyday Life

Just a few decades ago, artificial intelligence seemed like a concept straight out of science fiction. Today, AI is present in multiple aspects of our daily lives, often without us even realizing it.

From virtual assistants on our phones to the algorithms that determine which series we are recommended on streaming platforms, AI has become a key tool in modern society. In this chapter, we will explore how AI is transforming the way we interact with technology and how it facilitates our daily activities.

5.1 Virtual Assistants and Chatbots: AI as a Digital Companion

One of the most visible advances of AI in our daily lives is the development of virtual assistants and chatbots. These programs use artificial intelligence to understand and respond to questions in natural language, making it easier to send messages, schedule reminders, and answer queries.

The Most Popular Virtual Assistants

Some of the most widely used virtual assistants include:

☐ **Siri (Apple):** Can answer questions, send messages, and perform tasks through voice commands.

☐ **Google Assistant:** Provides useful information, answers questions, and controls smart devices.

☐ **Alexa (Amazon):** Connected to home devices, it allows everything from playing music to controlling lights and appliances.

☐ **Cortana (Microsoft):** Integrated into Windows, it helps with task management and information searches.

These assistants improve over time through machine learning, adapting better to user needs.

Chatbots and Customer Service

Chatbots have revolutionized customer service, allowing companies to provide 24/7 support without the need for human intervention. Banks, airlines, and online stores use chatbots to answer frequently asked questions and solve basic problems.

💡 *Example:* Companies like Sephora and H&M have implemented chatbots that help customers choose products based on their preferences.

5.2 AI in Entertainment: Music, Movies, and Video Games

AI has changed the way we consume entertainment, personalizing experiences and optimizing content production.

Recommendation Algorithms in Streaming

Services like Netflix, Spotify, and YouTube use AI to recommend content based on each user's habits.

💡 *Example:* If you watch a lot of science fiction movies on Netflix, its algorithm will suggest more similar content based on the preferences of other users with similar tastes.

AI in Music and Film Production

AI is also being used to create music and edit films. Some tools include:

☐ **Jukebox (OpenAI):** Can generate complete songs with vocals and instrumental accompaniment.

☐ **Adobe Sensei:** Uses AI to enhance video and photo editing.

☐ **Deepfake and Visual Effects:** AI allows face modification in movies and the creation of realistic special effects.

AI in Video Games

Video games have integrated AI to improve gameplay and enhance the player experience.

💡 *Example:* Games like *The Last of Us Part II* use advanced AI to make enemies react more realistically.

5.3 AI in Healthcare: Diagnosis and Well-being

One of the fields where AI has had the most positive impact is medicine and well-being. Thanks to its ability to analyze vast amounts of data, AI has improved disease diagnosis and personalized treatments.

AI-Assisted Diagnosis

AI is used to detect diseases with greater accuracy and speed.

☐ **DeepMind Health:** Identifies eye diseases through medical imaging.

☐ **IBM Watson Health:** Analyzes medical records to assist in disease diagnosis and treatment.

☐ **AI in Cancer Detection:** Algorithms have proven to be as effective as doctors in identifying cancer cells in mammograms.

Health and Well-being Applications

There are AI-based applications that help people maintain a healthy lifestyle.

💡 *Example:*

MyFitnessPal: Uses AI to recommend diet and exercise plans.

Sleep Cycle: Monitors sleep patterns and suggests improvements.

Woebot: An AI-based chatbot designed to provide psychological support.

5.4 AI in the Home: Smart Homes and the Internet of Things (IoT)

The integration of AI with home devices has led to smart home automation, making it easier to control appliances using voice commands or mobile applications.

Most Common Smart Devices

☐ **Smart Thermostats (Nest, Ecobee):** Adjust temperature based on the user's routine.

☐ **Smart Lights (Philips Hue):** Allow lighting adjustments via smartphone or voice assistants.

☐ **AI-Powered Security Cameras:** Analyze movement patterns and send alerts in case of suspicious activity.

💡 *Example:* If a user arrives home at the same time every day, AI can learn this pattern and automatically turn on the lights and adjust the temperature.

5.5 AI in Education: Personalized Learning

The education sector has also been transformed by AI, allowing for more personalized and accessible learning experiences.

AI-Based Educational Platforms

☐ **Duolingo:** Uses AI to adapt lessons based on user progress.

☐ **Khan Academy:** Provides personalized tutoring through machine learning algorithms.

☐ **Coursera and edX:** Online learning platforms that recommend courses based on user interests.

Automated Assessments and Virtual Tutors

AI also facilitates exam and assignment grading, as well as the development of virtual tutors that answer student questions in real time.

💡 *Example:* In China, some schools have implemented AI systems to analyze students' attention levels during classes.

Conclusion

AI has transformed our daily lives in ways that, just a few years ago, seemed unimaginable. From the way we interact with technology to how we consume entertainment, take care of our health, and learn, AI has become an essential tool for improving our quality of life.

However, its integration also presents challenges, such as data privacy and technological dependence. As AI continues to advance, it is crucial to find a balance between innovation and responsible use.

Chapter 6: The Future of AI and Its Impact on Society

Artificial intelligence has evolved from an emerging technology to a fundamental pillar of modern society. Its progress over the past decades has been impressive, but the road ahead is just as fascinating.

What will the future of AI look like? Will it reach levels of intelligence similar to humans? Will it displace millions of workers or create new job opportunities? What will be the ethical and legal limits?

In this chapter, we will explore the most relevant projections about the future of artificial intelligence and its impact on society.

6.1 General AI: Are We Close to Human-Level Intelligence?

So far, artificial intelligence has been mostly "narrow," meaning it is designed for specific tasks (such as image recognition, text translation, or playing chess). However, scientists are working on developing **Artificial General Intelligence (AGI)**, capable of matching or even surpassing human intelligence in any field.

Differences Between Weak AI, Strong AI, and General AI

☐ **Weak AI (or Narrow AI):** Designed for specific tasks (e.g., virtual assistants or recommendation algorithms).

☐ **Strong AI:** Advanced systems that can learn and reason similarly to humans but still have limitations.

☐ **Artificial General Intelligence (AGI):** AI with cognitive abilities comparable to those of a human, capable of reasoning, planning, and making decisions in multiple domains.

When Could We Achieve AGI?

Some experts believe that AGI could be developed in the coming decades, while others argue that we are still far from it due to challenges in language understanding, creativity, and reasoning.

💡 *Example:* OpenAI and DeepMind are working on increasingly advanced AI systems, such as GPT and AlphaFold, which demonstrate reasoning abilities close to human-level intelligence in specific tasks.

However, the development of AGI raises ethical and control dilemmas that have yet to be resolved.

6.2 AI and the Future of Employment: Ally or Threat?

One of the biggest debates surrounding AI is its impact on the job market.

Industries That Will Be Transformed by AI

Some industries are at risk of automation, while others could benefit from new job opportunities.

☐ **Jobs at Risk of Automation:**
- **Transportation** (taxis, autonomous trucks)
- **Customer service** (chatbots and virtual assistants)
- **Finance and accounting** (data analysis algorithms)
- **Manufacturing and production** (robots in factories)

☐ **New Job Opportunities:**
- **AI and machine learning engineers**
- **AI ethics and regulatory specialists**
- **Developers of robotics and autonomous systems**
- **Cybersecurity specialists**

How to Adapt to the AI-Driven Job Market?

To navigate this transformation, job retraining and continuous education in digital skills will be essential.

💡 *Example:* Countries like Finland have implemented free AI education programs to help citizens adapt to this new technological era.

6.3 AI and Its Impact on the Global Economy

Economic Growth Driven by AI

AI could boost productivity and generate trillions of dollars in global wealth. It is estimated that by 2030, AI will contribute over $15 trillion to the world economy.

Automation vs. Inequality

While AI can generate prosperity, it could also widen the gap between developed and developing countries, as not all nations have the same access to technology.

💡 *Example:* Companies like Google and Tesla invest billions in AI, while many countries still lack the infrastructure to leverage these technologies.

6.4 AI in the Future of Education

Personalized Learning Through AI

AI will enable more personalized education, adjusting the pace of teaching to each student.

☐ *Example:* Platforms like Khan Academy and Duolingo already use AI to tailor content based on student performance.

Virtual Reality and AI-Driven Simulations

Students could learn through interactive simulations and augmented reality.

💡 *Example:* Medical students could train using AI-powered surgical simulations before operating on real patients.

6.5 Risks and Challenges of AI's Future

As AI evolves, concerns about its potential risks arise.

AI and Data Privacy

The widespread use of AI could compromise people's privacy, as companies collect vast amounts of data.

💡 *Example:* Facebook's AI has been criticized for analyzing user behavior to influence political elections.

AI Regulation and Control

Governments and international organizations must establish regulations to ensure AI is used ethically and safely.

☐ **Possible Solutions:**
• Creation of global regulatory bodies for AI.
• Laws limiting the use of AI in mass surveillance.
• Development of explainable and auditable AI systems.

6.6 AI and the Concept of Technological Singularity

Some experts believe that AI could evolve to a point known as **"technological singularity,"** where its ability to improve itself would accelerate beyond human control.

What Is the Singularity?

The singularity is the moment when AI becomes more intelligent than humans and begins to improve itself without human intervention.

💡 *Example:* Ray Kurzweil, futurist and director of engineering at Google, predicts that singularity will occur around 2045.

Should We Be Concerned About the Singularity?

Some scientists believe that AI will remain a controlled tool, while others warn about the risks of AI evolving beyond human control.

Conclusion

The future of AI is full of promises and challenges. It could enhance productivity, personalize education, and revolutionize medicine, but it also raises dilemmas regarding privacy, inequality, and employment.

The key will be to find a balance between innovation and regulation, ensuring that AI benefits humanity as a whole.

Final Conclusion

Artificial intelligence has transitioned from a science fiction concept to one of the most influential technologies of our time. Throughout this book, we have explored its origins, how it works, its applications across different sectors, and its impact on society.

A Journey Through AI

From its mathematical and computational foundations to its integration into everyday life, AI has evolved rapidly. Today, it is used in healthcare, education, entertainment, security, and many other fields, improving efficiency and expanding human capabilities.

We have seen how AI is transforming the job market—automating repetitive tasks while also creating new professional opportunities. However, this technological revolution is not without challenges, including data privacy, ethical regulation, and its impact on economic inequality.

The Future of AI: Opportunities and Risks

The future of artificial intelligence is promising, but it also raises fundamental questions. To what extent can AI improve our lives without affecting our autonomy? How can we ensure its development is safe and equitable?

As we advance toward more sophisticated systems, it is crucial for governments, businesses, and citizens to work together to define the ethical and legal boundaries of AI. Transparency, fairness, and democratic access to technology will be essential to harness its potential while avoiding unnecessary risks.

Final Reflection

Artificial intelligence is not just a technological tool; it is a reflection of our choices as a society. Its development and use will depend on the direction we give it.

If we use it responsibly, creatively, and purposefully, AI can become a powerful ally for humanity, enhancing our abilities and helping us solve some of the world's most complex problems.

The future of AI is not yet written. It is up to us to decide how we want this technology to shape our lives.

Glossary of Key Terms

- **Artificial Intelligence (AI):** The ability of machines to perform tasks that typically require human intelligence, such as learning, reasoning, and problem-solving.

- **Machine Learning (ML):** A branch of AI that enables systems to learn from data and improve performance without explicit programming.

- **Neural Networks:** Computational models inspired by the human brain, used in deep learning to recognize patterns and process data.

- **Deep Learning:** A subset of machine learning that uses neural networks with multiple layers to analyze complex data.

- **Natural Language Processing (NLP):** The field of AI that allows computers to understand, interpret, and generate human language.

- **Computer Vision:** AI technology that enables machines to interpret and analyze images and videos.

- **Weak AI (Narrow AI):** AI systems designed for specific tasks, such as virtual assistants or recommendation algorithms.

- **Strong AI:** Advanced AI that can learn and reason similarly to humans but still has limitations.

- **Artificial General Intelligence (AGI):** A hypothetical AI capable of human-like reasoning and decision-making across multiple domains.
- **Algorithm:** A set of rules or instructions that AI systems follow to process data and make decisions.
- **Big Data:** Extremely large datasets that AI and machine learning models analyze to identify patterns and trends.
- **Chatbot:** An AI-powered program that interacts with users through text or voice to answer questions and provide assistance.
- **Automation:** The use of AI and robotics to perform tasks without human intervention.
- **Ethical AI:** The study and implementation of AI systems that consider fairness, transparency, and social impact.
- **Singularity:** A theoretical point at which AI surpasses human intelligence and begins improving itself autonomously.